Clothes Pegs at Dawn!

by

Brian Bennett

with illustrations by

Peter Dunn

Clothes Pegs at Dawn!
Brian Bennett

All Rights Reserved.

Copyright © 2023 Brian Bennett
Illustrations © Peter Dunn

Brian Bennett has asserted his moral right
to be identified as the author of this work.

The right of Brian Bennett to be identified as the author
of this work has been asserted in accordance with
Section 77 of the Copyright, Designs and Patents Act 1988.

This book is sold subject to the condition that it shall not, by way of trade or otherwise,
be lent, resold, hired out or otherwise circulated without the publisher's prior consent
in any form of binding or cover other than that in which it is published and without a
similar condition including this condition being imposed on the subsequent purchaser.

ISBN 979-8-8-660650-8-0

THIS BOOK IS

DEDICATED TO VIOLET

Can you see the fairy? She is hiding from me.
Is that her hiding in the tree?

Watch out Mr Spider, you'd better run quick!
Because I am going to hit you with my big stick.

Toot-toot, Toot-toot
Can you see the naughty gnome hiding in the fruit?

The lady opens her mouth to shout,

Telling the sleeping gnome, that he must get out,

But Paddy the naughty gnome does not care,

As he lifts his right leg into the air.

The farting fairy comes up with a plan.
Can you see the face of the little old man?

The naughty gnome looks at the cakes,
he can't make up his mind which one to take.

The fairy cakes are displayed on a stand,
the naughty gnome pulls the switch with his left hand.

Come on Anna eat your beans,

Remember that beans beans are good for your heart,

Remember that beans beans make you fart.

The naughty gnome takes a fall.
Can you count the black spots on the ball?

As the lady looks over the garden gate.
Can you see the naughty gnome lying in wait?

Is that a real gnome that I can see?
It looks like he is laughing at me.

GET BACK SPIDER. It's super gnome!
I am rescuing the fairy and taking her home.

The old farmer is thinking about his dancing pig, while he is watching some gnomes doing the jig.

Anna flies her red kite,
As the farting fairy farts with all her might,
The tortoise and the ladybird take a rest,
The bees are flying around their nest.

Mr and Mrs Jones are trying to sing a song,
All the time watching their gnomes dancing along.

The little girl holds on to her red kite,
To fly her kite, the farting fairy will have to fart with all her might.

The naughty gnome is stuck up a tree,
All the time he's being attacked by some angry bees.

Through the garden spreads the smelly fart,
Can you see the pretty bird sat on the cart?

The naughty gnome is lying still,
As she uses her long body to send a chill.

Perpperity, perppetity, pert,
That smelly fart really hurt,
Anna has to hold her nose,
As up in the air that smelly fart goes.

PPPPEEERRTTYY

As the girl dreams about her friend the farting fairy,
The dancing gnome is very hairy.

Mr and Mrs Jones are off to the shop,

Every now and then they have to stop,

It will take them a long time to make it home,

Followed closely by the naughty gnome.

The big brown dog has caught a rat,
He's holding the rat down on a green and black mat.

Splish, splosh what a lovely sound to make,
The naughty gnome smashes every cake,
He just could not care less,
Because he just likes to be naughty and make a mess.

Wake-up, wake-up shouts Paddy,
I must tell you about my magical grandaddy.

The lambs and the pig dance along,
As the horse and the chickens sing a song,
The four cows dance in a line,
As the naughty gnome waves his arms in time.

I may be only a purple pig,
But when I sing my song,
The naughty gnome must do a jig,
Jumping high in the air as he dances along.

More books by Brian Bennett are available now!
Look out for:

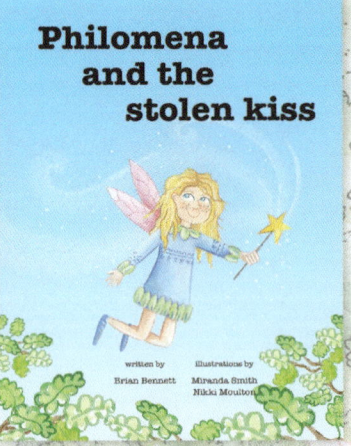

Philomena and the Stolen Kiss

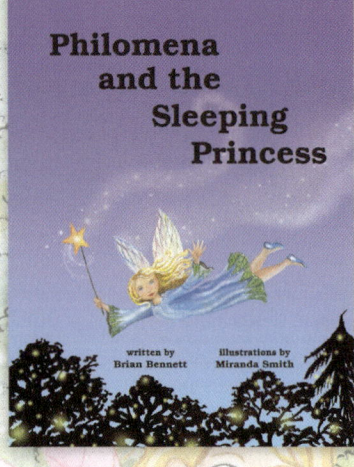

Philomena and the Sleeping Princess

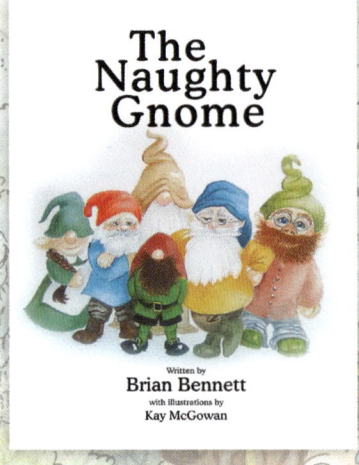

The Naughty Gnome

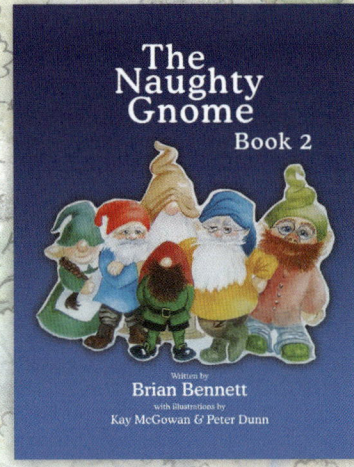

The Naugthy Gnome Book 2

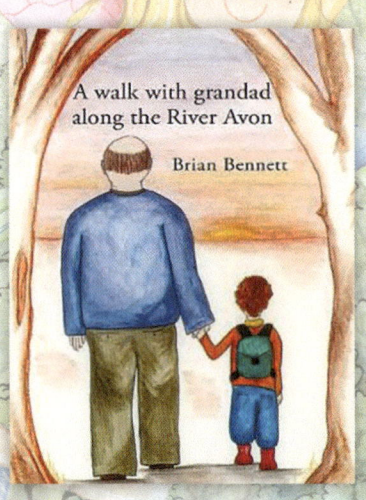

A walk with Grandad along the River Avon

Zolem

BRIAN BENNETT BOOKS

www.brianbennettbooks.com

ABOUT THE AUTHOR

Brian is a new author, he is a long-term dialysis patient of over 20 years and uses his 4 weekly sessions of treatment to write his many different genres of books.

Born in the mid 50s, Brian is a disabled man with a lifelong passion for angling, when his illness forced his retirement, he discovered his creative imagination, which shows in his love of writing.

Printed in Great Britain
by Amazon